PARASITIC PLANTS

PROFESSOR ERNST W. BAUER

TRANSLATED BY ALFRED LEUTSCHER

FRANKLIN WATTS LIMITED
26 Albemarle Street, London W.1

© 1975 Verlag J. F. Schreiber   SBN 85166 672 8
This edition: Illustrations © 1978 Verlag J. F. Schreiber
Text © Franklin Watts Limited 1978
First published by Verlag J. F. Schreiber, West Germany, under the
title *Pflanzenwelt voller Wunder*   Printed in Italy

2

A detailed look at the parasitic plants that live on other plants, and plants, such as pitchers, sundews and trappers, that catch food. The book concludes with a description of the primitive one-celled algae and suggests how similar ancestors evolved from one-celled forms to the present many-celled plants.

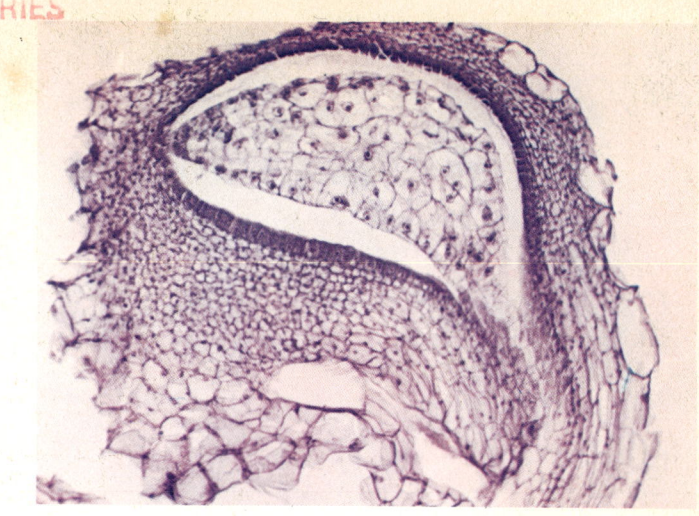

(opposite, left)
The Broomrape does not make its own foodstuff, and relies entirely on other plants. The microscope section *(right)* shows how the roots have penetrated the host plant. The Broomrape grows hardly any leaves. Its roots attach themselves to a host plant, from which it gets nourishment *(bottom, right)*.

In summer the brown shoots of the Broomrape appear on the woodland floor. A botanist considers it to be a flowering plant which is closely allied with carnivorous plants. It is not coloured green. Only the slender tips of its leaves and stalks contain a little leaf green, and are of little use in nourishing a healthy plant. The Broomrape has a well deserved name, since it lives entirely at the expense of another plant such as Clover. It is just as well that these parasites are far exceeded in numbers by their hosts, for this close relationship of the Broomrape would appear almost to be a "crime", so far as its feeding habit is concerned.

In the cases of the Eyebright and the Yellow Rattle (both parasitic plants), they have well developed green leaves, and can manufacture a certain amount of food themselves. Even so, they will attach themselves to other plants and feed on them.

To uncover the habits of the Broomrape, it is necessary to dig into the soil. The Dodder, on the other hand, makes its attack in the open air

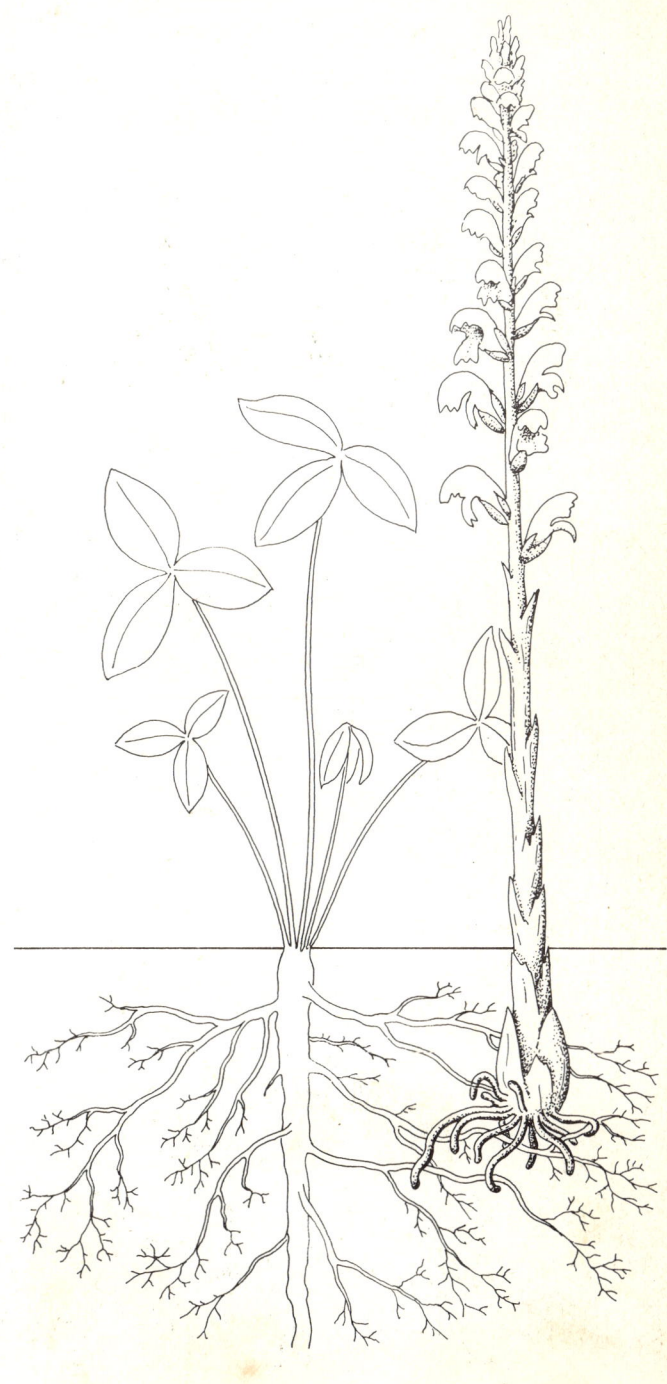

3

4

The Dodder *(below, left)* is an impressive parasite which entangles its host, and attaches itself by means of suckers. It has no leaves and relies on the host for food. The microscope photograph and sketch *(right)* show the connection. The upper section is the Dodder and the lower the host plant.

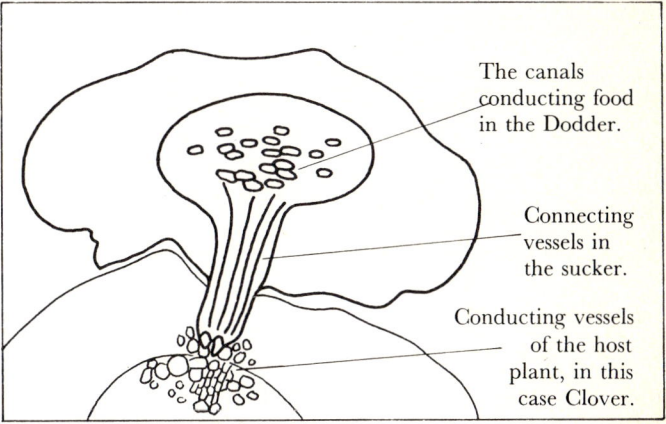

The canals conducting food in the Dodder.

Connecting vessels in the sucker.

Conducting vessels of the host plant, in this case Clover.

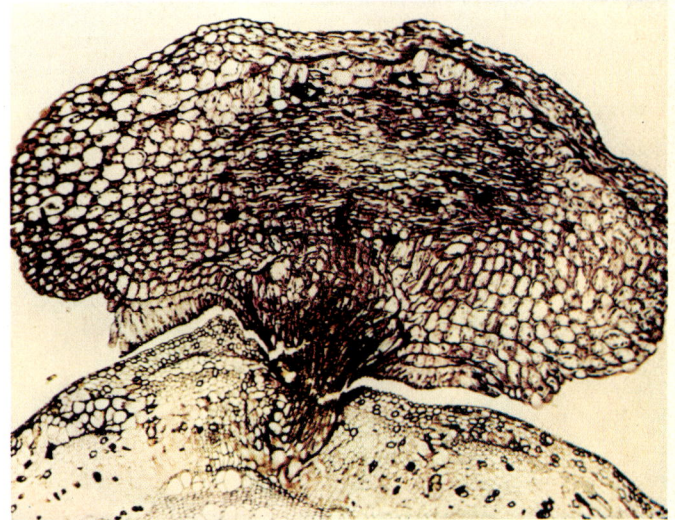

and sunshine. Like its near relatives the Bindweeds, it winds around the stems of its host. These are mostly Grasses or Stinging Nettles. Since it favours these plants with its tough and silky branches, it is sometimes called the Grass-, Nettle-, or Silk-spinner. In contrast to the bindweed, it does not attempt to grow upwards in order to reach the light. At intervals it attacks itself to its host by means of nipple-like swellings from which suckers penetrate in order to take

5

(opposite left, and below)
In this enlargement the ominous beauty of the
glandular hairs of the Sundew are clearly shown. On
these many insects come to grief *(below, right)*.
Possibly they mistake the glands for honeydew. This
is where death lurks for them, and all that is finally
left is an empty skin.

in water and food. Without this method of obtaining nourishment, the Dodder could not survive.

Just as remarkable as this plant parasite (and a group to which many toadstools belong) are the insectivorous plants. They are far smaller in size than horror films seem to suggest, and cannot possibly swallow a large animal, let alone a human being. They are,

The Sundew is found in many parts of the world. On the left is a long-leaved Sundew, and on the right a species which grows a tight rosette.

(bottom, left)
The layers of peat on a moorland hill build up year by year. The Sundew keeps pace with the surface by growing a fresh rosette each year. By following the successive rosettes downwards, it is possible to work out a chronological calendar of the moorland.

(opposite, right)
This Sundew leaf has captured a fly.

however, among the most attractive and interesting plants to study.

The name of the "Sundew" makes this obvious. When small insects,

presumably in search of nectar, are attracted by the sundew's shiny, scented glands, and land on its leaves, this could lead to their death. The plant's glandular hairs secrete a sticky glue, and can also curl around the victim. Like a many-fingered hand, the leaf twines itself around its prey.

On being captured, the insect does not survive long. The sundew's glands contain juices which can dissolve all the available contents of the insect and "digest" it. Not only do these glands trap and dissolve the insect, but they can also remove its food contents and pass these on to the plant.

In this manner such plants as the

The Butterwort looks quite harmless. A closer look reveals small dark spots which are empty bodies of insects, mostly ants. As soon as a small animal walks onto a leaf, it is held fast *(top picture)*. During the flowering season the often ignored butterwort looks its best *(lower picture)*.

with the water supply, since tap water is not too satisfactory; it contains far too much chalk. Many plants are very sensitive to this mineral, especially those growing naturally on moorland where chalk is deficient.

sundew can survive in moorland surroundings where the living conditions are poor.

It is not recommended that a sundew be kept indoors, since it is difficult to give it the conditions it requires in a closed room. The atmosphere indoors is much drier than out on the moors, where the plants are surrounded by wet Bog mosses. Indoors, very soon you will notice that the glistening hairs are missing. One way to protect the plant is to cover it with a glass dome. However, this will change its natural conditions, since glass filters off the ultra-violet rays which the plant would normally receive outdoors. Care should also be taken

A trap is constructed on the leaf of this Pitcher Plant. Insects climb along the broad leaf stalk in order to reach the honey glands of the "pitcher" which are situated beneath the rim. In doing so, they slip and fall in, and are slowly digested. The food which is released is taken in through the walls of the pitcher.

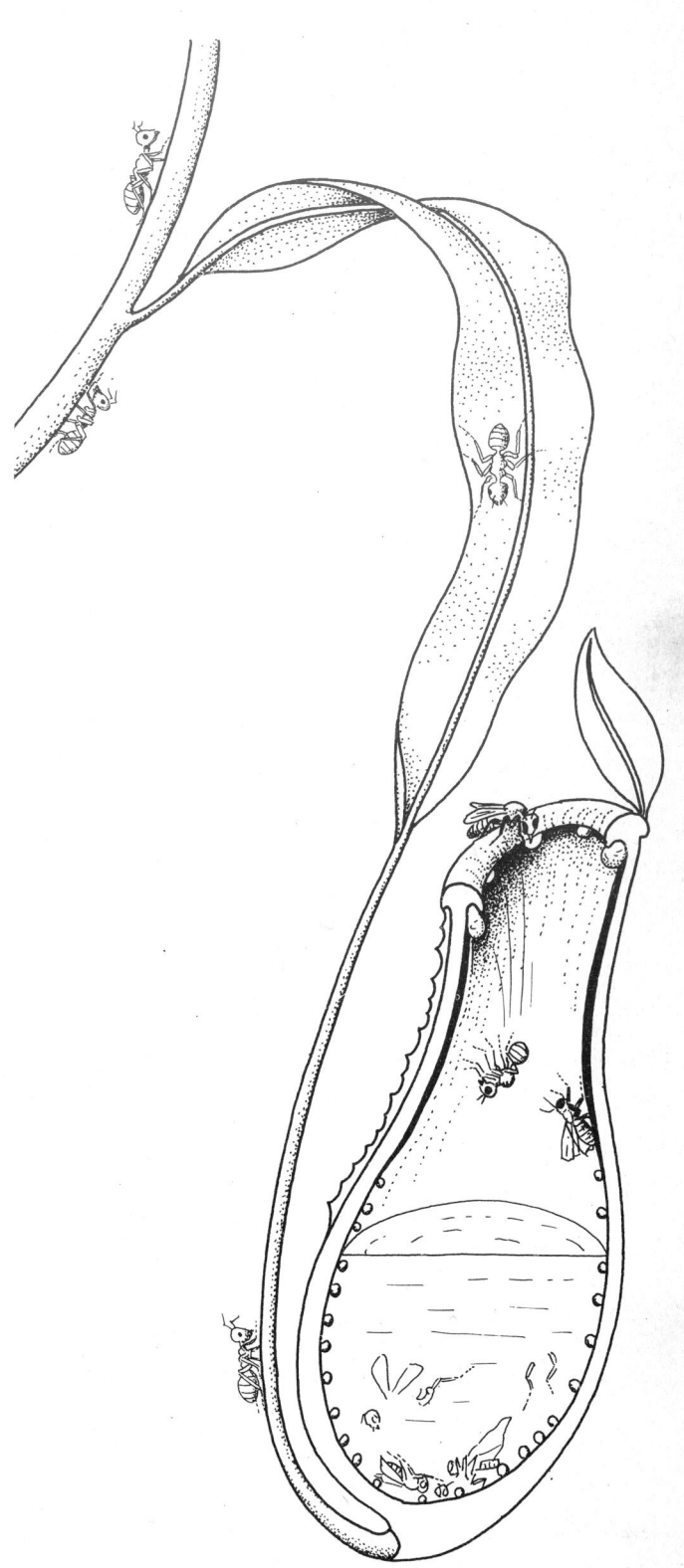

The Pitcher Plant has another method of deceiving nectar-seeking insects. Under the mirror-bright, swollen rim of its "pitcher" are situated its nectaries. An insect which climbs up the hairy side of the pitcher, seeking the honey inside the rim, comes into contact with the slippery edge, slides off and falls in. Its fate is sealed, since the bottom of the pitcher is filled with a digestive fluid, secreted by special glands at the base of the pitcher. Since the inside of the pitcher is smooth and covered with downward-pointing hairs, the insect has no chance of escaping from this trap.

Frequently there are animals which take advantage of such a trap. Spiders spin their webs across the pitcher, and literally "steal" the booty of insects from the very mouth of the pitcher. However, these spiders do not go unpunished, since there are birds which are ready to catch *them*. Actually, the spiders are, on the whole, little troubled by this, for they have the ability to hide in the pitcher plant's digestive juices, to which they are immune.

(opposite)
In Indonesia grows the Pitcher Plant *Nephenthes*. This beautiful creation is a death trap for insects.

The picture below shows the digestive glands at the base of the Pitcher under a microscope.

There is another reason which make the sundews scientifically renowned. They can be used in dating the age of a moorland. Year by year a new rosette will grow out from the previous one, a little higher up in order to keep pace with the rising moorland peat. Since a sundew has a long life, it is possible by digging deep enough to follow each successive annual stem to a considerable depth in the peat. If you dig down along each side of the main stem, following each buried plant, you can reach far into the past, even thousands of years. If a point is reached where the stem finally ends, this could be where the moorland peat first started to form.

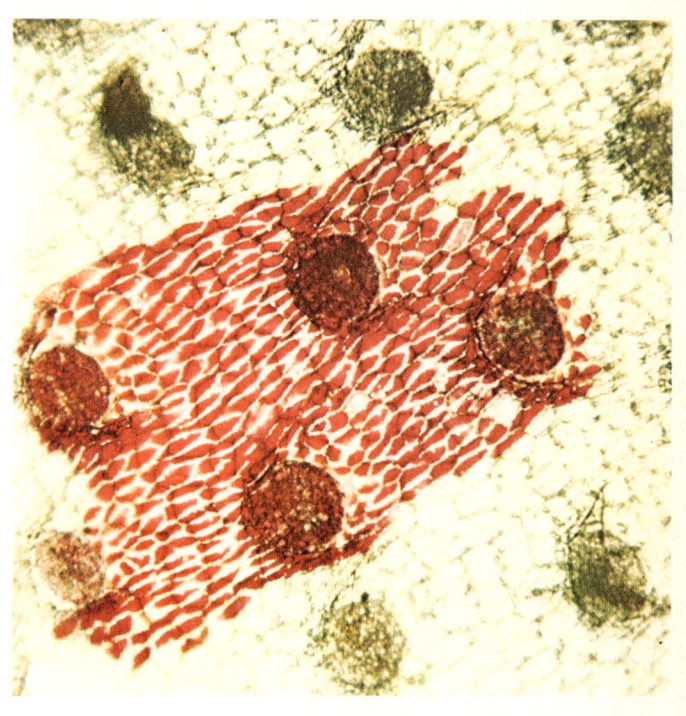

Another plant often found by the sundew is the Butterwort (page 10). What at first looks like a sticky layer on the leaves is really a surface of tiny, glandular hairs which act as a trap for insects. Small species, especially ants, walk over the leaves, stick tight and are digested. The leaf then curls inwards along its border, so as to catch dew or light rain which then washes the food over the leaf surface.

Pitcher plants occur widely in the virgin forests in tropical parts of southern Asia and in East Africa. In America some pitchers grow on the ground. They attract insects by their colours and markings around the mouth of the pitcher. Water lies at the bottom of the pitcher and in this insects drown and decompose. The food thereby released is taken in through the walls of the pitcher.

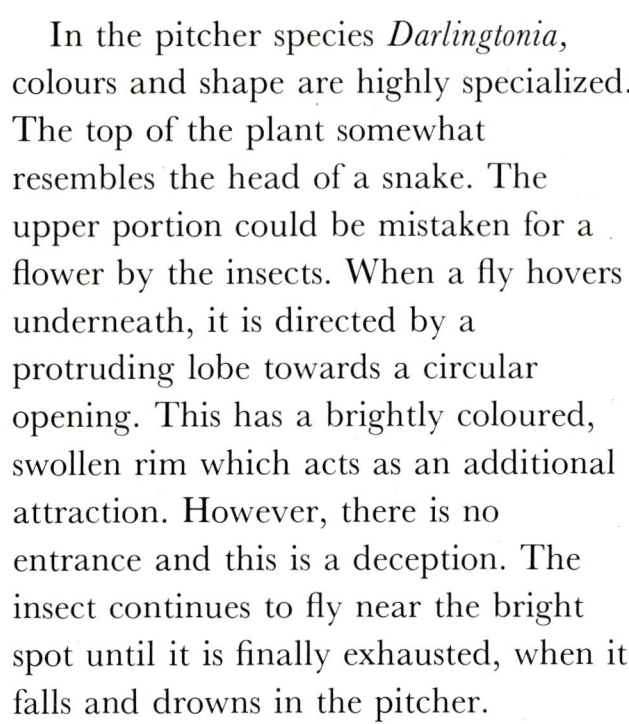

The leaves of the Californian Pipe Plant *Darlingtonia* *(top picture)* are very efficient light traps. The Pitcher Plant *Sarracenia* lives on moorlands in south-east North America *(bottom picture)*.

(opposite, right)
A ground Pitcher Plant, called *Cephaliotus*.

In the pitcher species *Darlingtonia*, colours and shape are highly specialized. The top of the plant somewhat resembles the head of a snake. The upper portion could be mistaken for a flower by the insects. When a fly hovers underneath, it is directed by a protruding lobe towards a circular opening. This has a brightly coloured, swollen rim which acts as an additional attraction. However, there is no entrance and this is a deception. The insect continues to fly near the bright spot until it is finally exhausted, when it falls and drowns in the pitcher.

When you think about this, it could appear as if the plant has "thought up" this idea, and deliberately built the trap. This is ridiculous, although it was once a popular belief. What applies to this trap also applies to any leaf or flower—in fact, to all forms of life. They have evolved over millions of years. Gradually, from generation to generation, life forms and colours have altered, and adapted themselves to survive.

A good example of this change can be found among the pollinating insects. In order to be sure of accomplishing their tasks, they must constantly readapt to new situations. It is the same with the insect traps. In tropical rain forests, insects are constantly drowning and decomposing in the water-filled pitcher plants, to be absorbed through the leaf surface. The slow evolution from a simple, hollow leaf, to a deep pitcher with glands and a digestive system, is understandable. Without the behaviour patterns of the insects, this would certainly never have come about.

Bristles on the surface of the leaf of the Venus Flytrap are sensitive to touch.

Not only do some plants behave in this "animal-like" fashion by making use of glandular hairs and pitchers. Through evolution others have developed their leaves into hinged traps. The *Aldrovana vesiculosa* (page 19), only rarely found in European lakes, can close up in a matter of 1/50 second. This high speed sets up a water current strong enough to sweep in water insects for the plant to feed on.

The Venus Flytrap is one of the types of insectivorous plants with trap-doors. In a fraction of a second the leaf snaps shut when the bristles on the inside are repeatedly touched. For the captive insect there is no escape.

Among land plants, this works with equal efficiency. The Venus Flytrap of North America has the two halves of its leaves standing at approximately right angles when at rest. Their borders are lined with teeth. In the centre of each half are three bristles. If repeatedly touched by an insect, the leaf closes with lightning speed, to become a perfect prison.

In trying to free itself, the insect disturbs the plant more and more, so that it remains tightly shut, holding its victim captive. Then, the numerous short, glandular hairs on the leaf surface come into operation, and quickly digest the captive.

That this rapid movement of the Venus Flytrap has attracted the attention of botanists is understandable. For some time it was believed that the closing of the leaf was due to some

Fishes are rivals of the Bladderwort, since they also hunt small crustaceans. Consequently, vegetarian fishes eating a bladderwort get an extra meal!

built-up pressure in the cells. As soon as the leaf is touched, pressure from the epidermal cells (on the outer skin layer) is released on the inner side, and the leaf snaps shut. Later, the outside of the leaf begins to swell in the region of the hinge, so that the leaf halves reopen once more in a few minutes.

There is a similarity between the flowers of the Sundew, the Flytrap and the *Aldrovana*. All three belong to the same family. Their carnivorous habit appears to be the common factor and, as a form of plant behaviour, is very unusual. Between pitcher plants, on the one hand, and sundews and flytraps, on the other, there is no essential difference. Whereas the brightly coloured pitchers such as *Darlingtonia* can catch prey without being touched, this is not the case with sundews and flytraps. In this case there has to be some contact, and the trap reacts accordingly.

For many years a search was made for some nerve mechanism in the sundew, but research was fruitless. Obviously these plants work in a special

This Bladderwort *Aldrovana* is very rare and can be recognised by the tiny bladders which are capable of catching small water animals.

tension so that the leaf and its glandular hairs close around the prey.

Another carnivorous plant is the Bladderwort which has highly specialized traps. A water flea attaches itself to a bladder-shaped leaf on the

way, yet there must be some communication between leaf and insect when contact is made. This seems to be the only area to look at, in order to understand the method of capture.

Every time the trigger hairs of the flytrap are touched, their sensitive cells react and they collapse. Probably they receive some stimulus which can spread through the leaf. As this accumulates, a tension builds up and the trap is sprung. In the case of the sundew's glandular hairs, they do not seem to receive much stimulus from the protein substances which occur in the skin of the insects, since they do not digest them and indeed proteins are already present in the plant cells. This causes a build-up of

The top drawing shows the bladder with its door shut. As soon a a water flea touches the bristles, it is sucked inside by the inward pressure of water. The rush of water carries it inside *(bottom drawing)*.

side branch of this submerged plant. What then occurs illustrates how remarkably this trap is constructed. Under the lens can be seen quite clearly many dark objects which turn out to be the remains of water fleas and springtails. How have they entered the bladder?

With patience and some element of luck this can be observed. Whenever a water flea approaches close enough to a bladder to touch the bristles near the opening, it suddenly disappears as if by magic. The next instant it is inside the the bladder. After the capture, the bladder very obviously swells up (before it appeared somewhat collapsed) in a similar way to that in which we can suck through a straw by exerting pressure with our cheeks.

Such a comparison helps to unravel the puzzle. The hair triggers of the Bladderwort help to create a kind of vacuum inside the bladders, which swell up by taking in water and so create a current. The door at the mouth of the bladder is so constructed that it closes under this pressure which sucks in the

prey, and at the same time holds the door tightly shut. The movement is so rapid that the naked eye cannot follow it. High-speed photography shows that the opening action takes about 1/60 second and that, after another 1/40

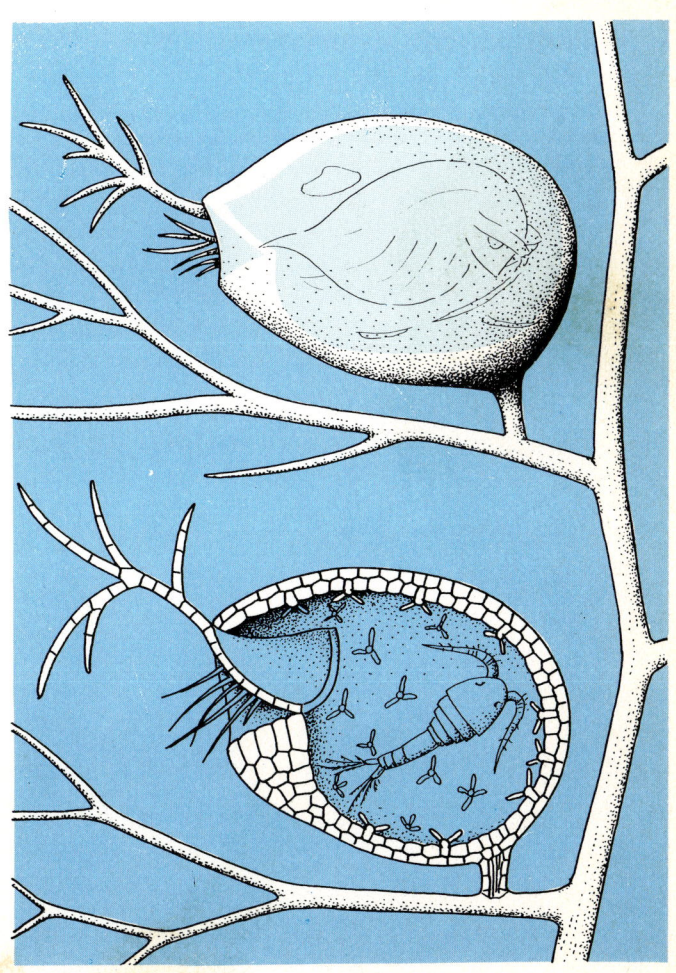

Only when the bladders have caught sufficient prey does the plant have enough strength to produce flowers.

At the end of April and beginning of May the Arum Lily flowers. Its hood entraps insects which are held captive for a few days. In the section through it *(bottom photograph)* you can see inside the chamber. Beneath the violet club-shaped inner stalk is a ring of bristles, and below this the small, reddish, male organs and the white female organs.

second, the door closes. Pressure inside the bladder has also been worked out, and equals about 0.35 atmospheres (an atmosphere = pressure at 15lb per square inch). Such detailed measurement is not really important, although interesting, since it is possible to see this phenomenon by careful observation with the naked eye.

By taking a plant out of water you can hear a faint rustling as the bladders open up and take in some air. Return the plant to the water and the traps close again. You can see them swell up as the internal pressure builds up. When the ultimate pressure is reached, the door opens.

It has often been asked whether the capture of prey is important to these plants. If a sundew is kept under glass to prevent any ants from crawling over the leaves, then it seems to lack something. It grows more slowly and remains small. Also, a bladderwort minus bladders will not grow any flowers.

Among these "trapdoor" plants belongs the wild Arum Lily, whose

This plant also has pitcher-shaped organs, which trap insects for a short while. However, there is food for them since the wall of the flask has nectar-secreting glands. The photograph below shows a species from Chile. The very ornamental species on the opposite page comes from America.

attracted by the unpleasant smell which the arum emits. They fly towards it and, on settling, slip down the sides of the hood which is covered with droplets of oil. (They have no difficulty in pushing through the narrow passage, although it is blocked by a close-fitting circle of bristles, in order to reach the interior of the hood.) In time a number of insects get to this inner chamber where the floral parts are situated. Blundering about, they transfer pollen onto the stigmas. Escape would seem impossible, since the slippery wall of the hood is hard to scale. Also, there are bristles which prevent any exit.

After fertilization has taken place, the stamens ripen (in about two days' time) and cover the insects with pollen. The bristles inside the hood wither and collapse, and the slippery wall dries up. Escape is now possible. Covered in pollen, many of the escaped prisoners make straightaway for another arum flower, and are once again trapped.

This situation for the insects is, however, not without some advantage, since the temperature inside the hood can reach

flower is covered by a hood. This is a temporary trap, which lasts only as long as, and until, the flower of the plant is pollinated by the captive insects. Tiny flies and beetles are

In mineral-rich ponds can be found the free-swimming *Euglena*. It consists of a single cell containing green chloroplasts, and a long flagellum at the front.

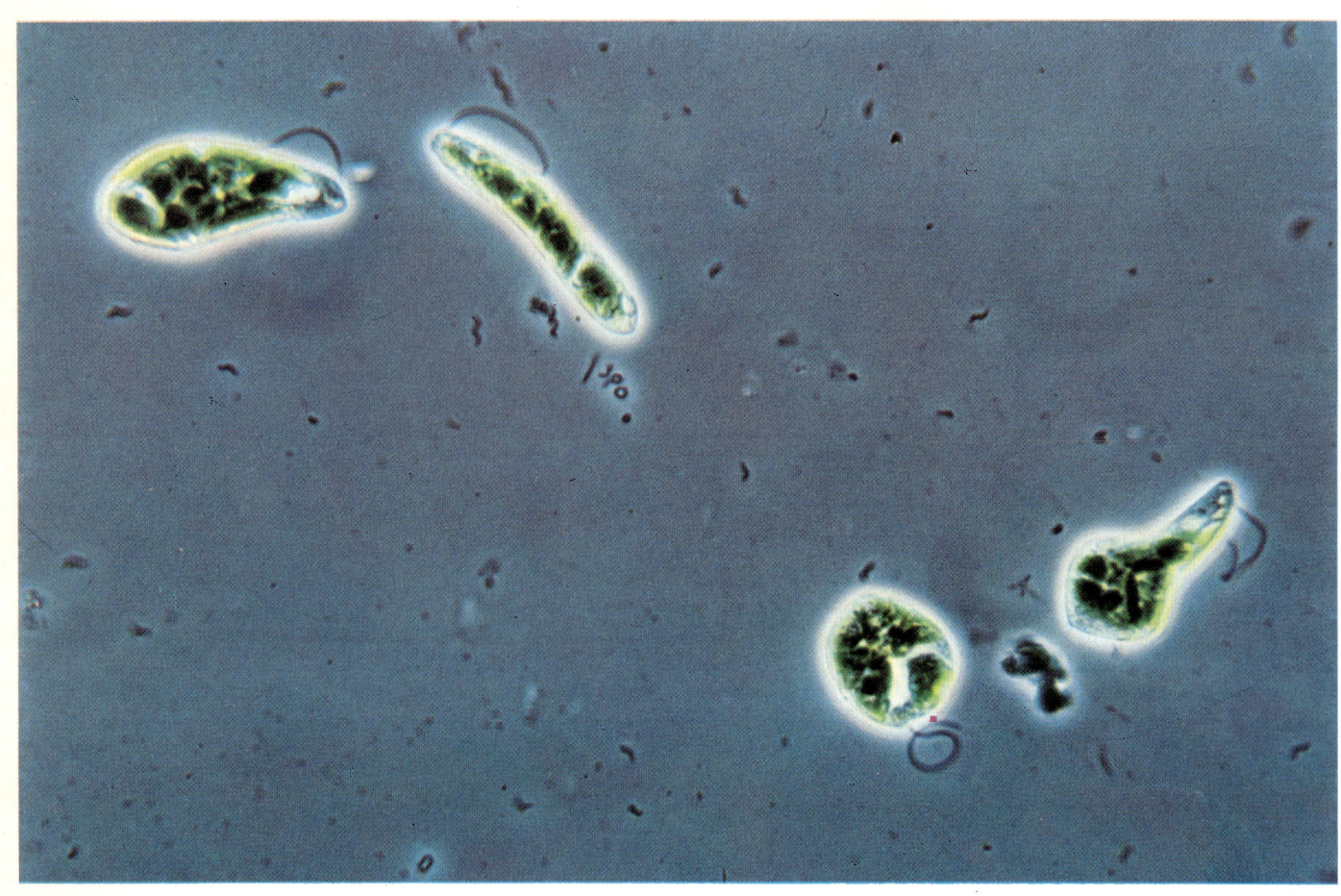

16 degrees higher than outside. During a cold May night this is obviously an advantage.

Many other plants have similar flowers which trap small flies, and release them after a few days. Although not closely related they behave in a similar fashion. This is of benefit to the insects, since during their temporary imprisonment they are repaid with food and warmth.

This close relationship between plants and animals must have evolved over a very long period. Some 300,000 million years ago, only plants existed on earth, and these plants consisted of only a

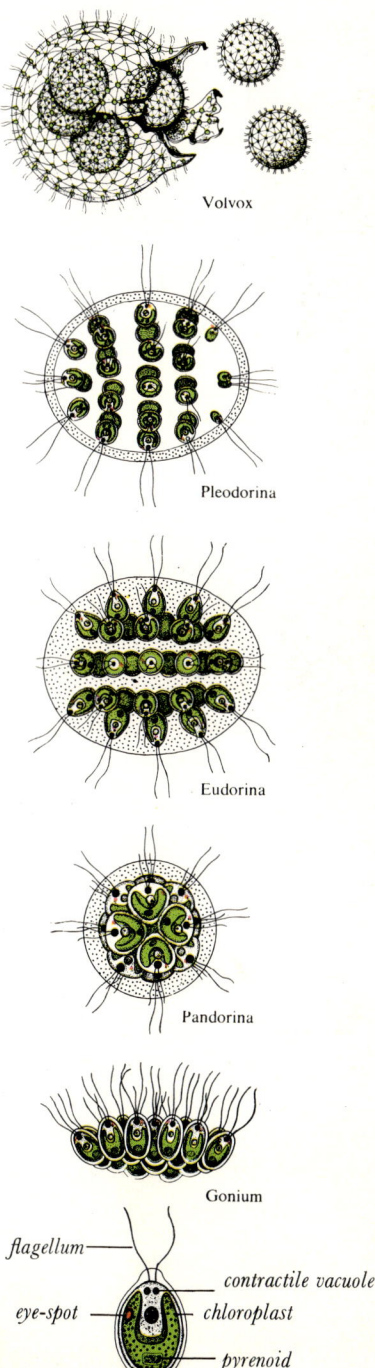

Volvox

Pleodorina

Eudorina

Pandorina

Gonium

flagellum

eye-spot

contractile vacuole

chloroplast

pyrenoid

single, or at most a few, cells. From such dwarf ancestors the whole diverse plant kingdom has evolved, consisting today of some 380,000 species. These first plants differed from even earlier ancestors, in possessing something which previously did not occur in living things. This was the appearance of the green colouring matter, chlorophyll, which enables plants to use the sun's energy in making their own food. This process is called "photosynthesis". With the sun's help they can utilize the carbon dioxide, water and salts to build up their own food supply. Not only can they utilize this themselves but also provide food for animals and man.

The first ancestors of plants probably existed in the sea. Today both salt and freshwater algae occur. Many, such as the little *Euglena,* are active. It uses a thread (or flagellum) at its front end to pull itself through the water propellorwise.

Some old forms of algae have in course of time evolved to become multi-cellular. In the species *Eudorina* there are some 32 cells gathered into a hollow

This colonial alga, *Eudorina*, consists of cells which are embedded in a jelly envelope.

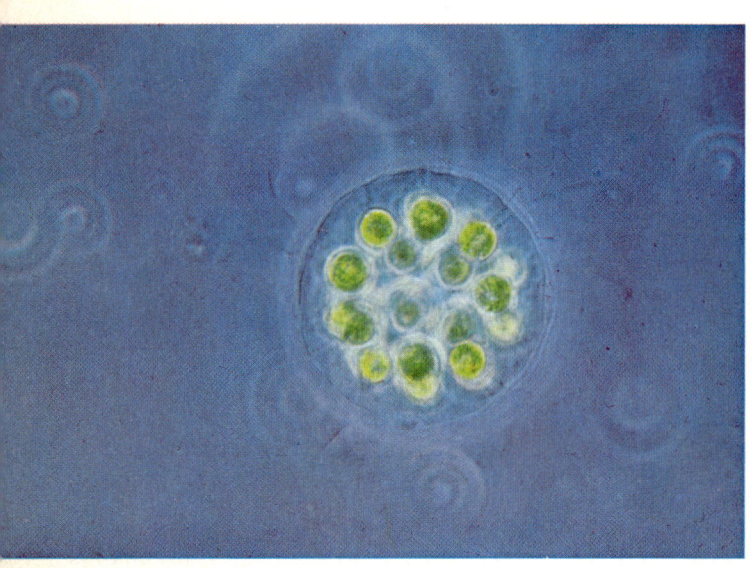

two. Being able to produce leaves, stalks and flowers requires many different kinds of cell structure. In a Poppy there can be as many as 80 different cell tissues.

All this has taken a very long time to evolve. To see how this can work, it helps to study these tiny cell colonies and see whether they contain any different types of cell structure. In a species related to *Eudorina* with its 32 cells is a species called *Pleurodina*. When a cell-colony of this splits up, only 28 cells function. The other four remain small and eventually perish.

In another species, *Volvox*, there are up to 20,000 cells. They surround an inner space to form a kind of latticed outer sphere. In contrast to *Eudorina* and *Pleurodina*, where each cell is separately contained in a jelly envelope, those of *Volvox* are bound together. Some cells are noticeably larger, and are capable of reproducing. As soon as they reach a certain size, they split off into the hollow central chamber and begin dividing to produce further, multi-celled colonies.

sphere. It is probable that in the same manner as described below the one-celled kinds have changed into many-celled plants. Contact between these 32 cells of *Eudorina* are not very tight, and they are all similar. When they separate, each cell divides into 2, then 4, 8, 16, until again 32 cells are produced. They remain together as a colony until further separation and cell division takes place.

Although such simple forms of algae are undoubtedly plants, and so related to the higher flowering plants, there is an enormous difference between the

Volvox is one of the very beautiful and remarkable forms of colonial algae, consisting of cells which are joined together in a jelly-like coat, so as to form a hollow sphere. A few cells have the power to multiply. They separate into the hollow sphere *(lower picture)* and divide to form daugher colonies.

Branches of the Giant Kelp, a seaweed, can grow up to 40 metres long. Swim bladders are carried on the fronds.

(opposite, right)
From the single-celled algae to the flowering plants, such as this Corn Poppy, has been a very long process, lasting millions of years. From this have evolved, time and again, different kinds of shoots, leaves, roots and flowers.

The thread-like, filamentous algae are probably also derived from single-celled ancestors. Although their cells are joined, they can also divide. Larger algae such as seaweeds can attach themselves to the sea bed and become sedentary. In the ocean there are some giant kelps which reach a length of some 100 metres, and with fronds held up by bladders some five metres long.

The greatest adventure among plants was their invasion of the dry land. This must have acquired considerable adaptation—an ability to avoid drying up, the need for a firm shoot, a resistance to wind and weather, a system of conducting water, and roots which can draw up water from the soil and also give firm anchorage. This process took millions of years, even before the first plants became established on land, probably along the sea borders. From them all kinds of land plants have evolved.

For a while these daughter colonies remain inside the parent *Volvox*. Then, in a few days, the parent's outer envelope collapses, and the daughter colonies swim free. This is how *Volvox* multiplies. However, it is at some sacrifice, since the parent colony perishes. *Volvox* can also produce male and female cells, which can unite and subsequently divide into new plants.

However, despite all this we must not assume that all present-day plants have evolved from such algal colonies. They are merely examples of simple cell colonies which can perform different functions.

Photographs reproduced by courtesy of:

Ernst Bauer, 8 *(right)*, 10 *(left)*, 14, 16, 17, 23 *(top)*;
Dr. Heinz Schneider, 20 *(right)*, 26, 28, 29;
Heinz Schrempp, 2, 4, 8 *(left)*, 10 *(right)*, 12, 15,
19, 22, 23 *(bottom)*, 25; Fritz Schwäble, 7, 9;
V-Dia, 3, 5, 6, 13, 20 *(left)*, 24, 31

INDEX